Maryland

Experience Science

HOUGHTON MIFFLIN   BOSTON

Authors

William Badders
Director of the Cleveland
Mathematics and
Science Partnership
Cleveland Municipal
School District
Cleveland, Ohio

Douglas Carnine, Ph.D.
Professor of Education
University of Oregon
Eugene, Oregon

Bobby Jeanpierre, Ph.D.
Assistant Professor,
Science Education
University of Central Florida
Orlando, Florida

James Feliciani
Supervisor of Instructional
Media and Technology
Land O' Lakes, Florida

Carolyn Sumners, Ph.D.
Director of Astronomy
and Physical Sciences
Houston Museum
of Natural Science
Houston, Texas

Catherine Valentino
Author-in-Residence
Houghton Mifflin
West Kingston, Rhode Island

Printed in the U.S.A.

ISBN-13: 978-0-547-00879-0
ISBN 0-547-00879-1

1 2 3 4 5 6 7 8 9 RRD 14 13 12 11 10 09 08 07

Contents

Changes in the Sky

Contents

1 What Can You See in the Sky?

The day sky is light.
You may see clouds.
You may see birds.
You may see the Sun, too.

You may see other things
in the day sky.
Sometimes you can see
the Moon.
You may see a hot-air balloon.

The Day Sky

The **Sun** is the brightest object in the day sky.

It warms the land.

It warms the water.

It warms the air, too.

The Sun makes the sky bright.
You will not see other stars
in the day.

The Night Sky

The night sky is dark.
There is no light from the Sun.
You can see the Moon at night.
You can see stars, too.
A **star** is an object that makes
its own light.

Sometimes you can see planets.
A **planet** is an object that moves
around the Sun.
Earth is a planet.

Compare and Contrast

How are the day sky and
the night sky different?

9

2 What Causes Day and Night?

This girl is playing outside during the day.
The sky is light.

The sky is dark at night.
The girl needs a light to see
at night.

Day on Earth

Earth **rotates**, or spins.
The Sun shines on different parts
of Earth when Earth spins.

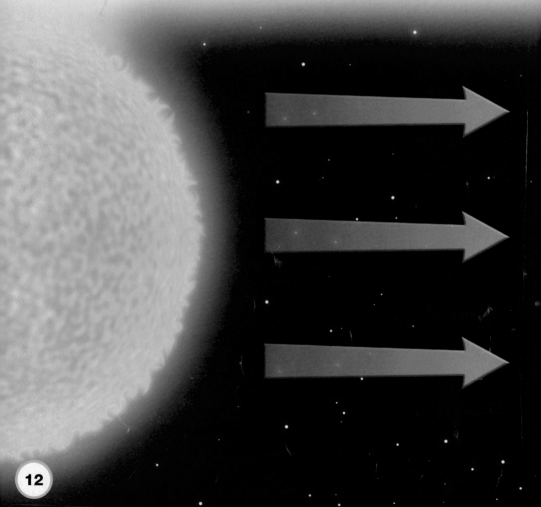

It is day when the part of Earth where you live faces the Sun.

day

Night on Earth

It is night when the part of Earth where you live faces away from the Sun.

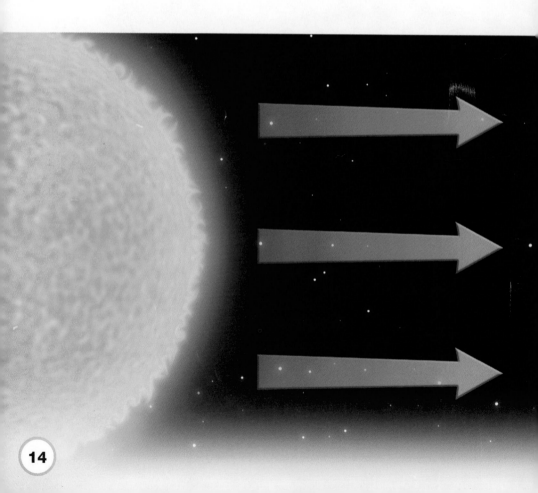

It takes 24 hours for Earth
to rotate one time.
Earth keeps rotating.
Day and night repeat.

Cause and Effect

Why is the sky dark at night?

night

3 How Does the Moon Seem to Change?

The **Moon** is an object close
to Earth.
You can see dark spots
on the Moon.
Some of these spots
are called craters.

The Sun is a star.
It makes its own light.
The Moon is not a star.
It does not make light.
We see the part of the Moon
that the Sun is shining on.

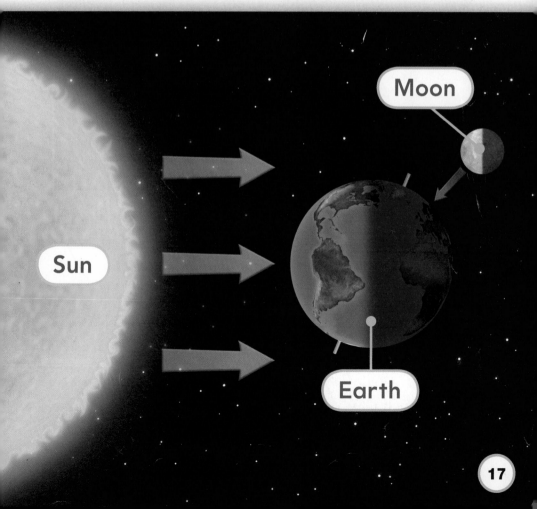

Moon

Sun

Earth

The Changing Moon

The Moon is round, but it seems to change.

The Moon's shape looks different every night.

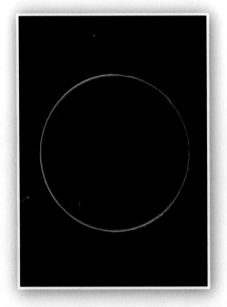

new moon

first quarter moon

The Moon moves around Earth.
It takes 28 days.
We see different parts
of the Moon as it moves.

full moon

last quarter moon

Cause and Effect

Why does the Moon
seem bright?

4 How Does the Sun Seem to Move?

The Sun seems to move from one side of the sky to the other.
The Sun is not moving.
Earth is moving.
Earth is rotating.

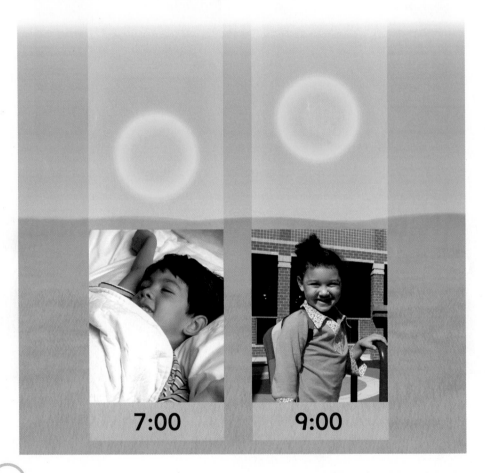

7:00   9:00

The Sun is low in the sky
in the morning.
It is high in the sky at noon.
It is low in the sky late
in the day.

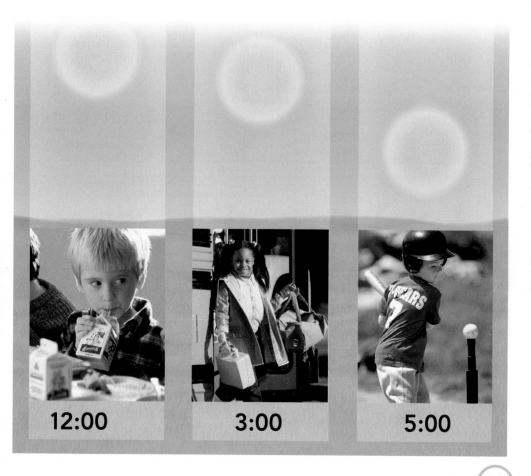

12:00   3:00   5:00

The Sun and Shadows

A **shadow** forms
when an object blocks light.
Shadows change during the day.

long shadow

short shadow

Shadows change
because the Sun is
in different parts of the sky.

long shadow

Draw Conclusions

**What happens to the Sun in
the sky as Earth rotates?**

Glossary

Moon A space object close to Earth.

planet A space object that moves around the Sun.

rotates Spins. Day and night happen when Earth rotates.

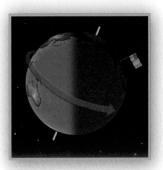

shadow Something that forms when an object blocks light.

Glossary

star A space object that makes its own light.

Sun The brightest space object in the day sky.

Think About What
You Have Read

1 A space object that moves around the Sun is _____.

A) a star

B) the Moon

C) the Sun

D) a planet

2 What can you see in the night sky?

3 What causes day and night?

4 How many times does Earth rotate in one week? How do you know?

Weather and Seasons

Contents

1 What Is Weather?

Weather is what the air outside is like.

There are many kinds of weather.

Weather may be warm or cool.

Weather may be sunny or cloudy.

warm and sunny

Weather may be windy.
Weather may be rainy, too.
You can see and feel weather.

windy

rainy

Ways Weather Changes

Monday	cloudy	
Tuesday	rainy	
Wednesday	sunny	

Weather Changes

Weather can change
from day to day.
One day may be sunny
and warm.
The next day may be cloudy
and cool.
Then clouds may bring rain.

Main Idea

What are some kinds
of weather?

2 How Can You Measure Weather?

You can use tools to tell about weather.
A **thermometer** is a tool that measures temperature.
Temperature is how warm or cool something is.

You can tell what to wear
by the temperature.
You wear warm clothes
when it is cold.
You wear clothes that keep you
cool when it is hot.

Tools for Wind and Rain

You can use a tool
to measure wind.
A windsock shows
which way the wind blows.
A windsock shows
how hard the wind blows.

windsock

You can use a tool
to measure rain.
A rain gauge measures
how much rain falls.

rain gauge

Draw Conclusions

What can you tell
about the wind if a windsock
is hanging down?

3 What Are Clouds and Rain?

Water moves from place to place.
The **water cycle** is when water moves from Earth to the sky and back again.

1 The Sun warms water.
Some warm water goes into the air.
You cannot see it.

2 Water in the air cools. Tiny drops of water make up a cloud.

3 Some drops get bigger. The drops fall back to Earth as rain.

Kinds of Clouds

There are many kinds of clouds.
Clouds have different shapes.
Clouds have different colors.
Look at clouds to see
how weather changes.
These clouds are thin.
It may rain in a day or two.

cirrus clouds

Some clouds are puffy and white.
They can turn gray and
bring rain.
Some clouds are low and gray.
They may bring rain or snow.

cumulus clouds

stratus clouds

Cause and Effect

What can clouds tell you
about changes in the weather?

4 What Is Weather Like in Spring and Summer?

A **season** is a time of year.
It has its own kind of weather.

Spring

Spring is the season
that follows winter.
It is warmer in spring.
Warmer weather and
spring rain help plants grow.

Animals find food
when new plants grow.
Animals that were sleeping
in winter wake up.
Many baby animals are born
in spring.

Summer

Summer is the season
that follows spring.
Summer is the warmest
season of the year.
People try to stay cool.
They wear clothing
that keeps them cool.

Plants grow in summer.
Young animals grow, too.
Young animals learn to find food.
This lamb eats a growing plant.

Compare and Contrast

How are spring and summer different?

5 What Is Weather Like in Fall and Winter?

Fall is the season
that follows summer.
It is cooler in fall.
People wear warmer clothes.
Leaves drop from some trees.

Animals get ready
for colder weather.
Some animals grow thick fur.
Other animals move
to places that have more food.
Many animals store food
for winter.

Winter

Winter is the season
that follows fall.
It is the coldest season
of the year.
Snow falls in some places.

Sometimes it is hard for animals to find food.
Some plants die.
Many trees lose their leaves.

The Pattern of Seasons

The seasons change in the same order every year.
The order is spring, summer, fall, and winter.

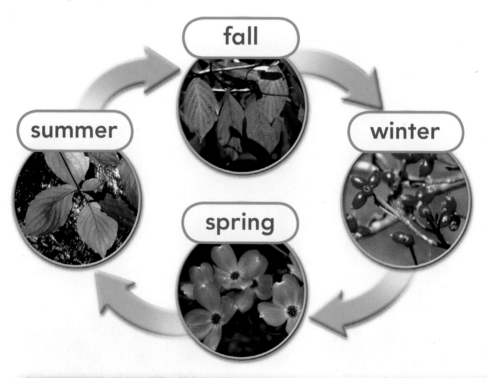

Sequence

What season comes before winter?

Glossary

cloud Many drops of water together.

fall The season that follows summer. In fall, the weather gets cooler.

season A time of year that has its own kind of weather.

spring The season that follows winter. Many baby animals are born in spring.

summer The season that follows spring. Summer is the warmest season.

Glossary

temperature How warm or cool something is. The temperature is cold when there is snow.

thermometer A tool that measures temperature.

water cycle Water moving from Earth to the sky and back again.

weather What the air outside is like.

winter The season that follows fall. Winter is the coldest season.

Think About What You Have Read

❶ A tool that measures temperature is called a _____.

A) cloud

B) summer

C) thermometer

D) winter

❷ What is a season?

❸ What can you tell by looking at clouds?

❹ How do you know it is windy if you cannot see the wind?

Water and Weather

Contents

1 How Does Water Change?

Water is part of weather.
Rain is water.
Rain falls from clouds.

Rain is a liquid.

Rain is wet.

Rain is clear.

water

Water Freezes

Water changes when
it gets very cold.
Water will freeze into ice
when it gets very cold.

ice

To **freeze** is to change
from a liquid to a solid.
Ice is a solid.
Ice is cold and hard.

ice

Ice Melts

Ice changes when it gets warm.
Ice will melt when it gets warm.
To **melt** is to change
from a solid to a liquid.

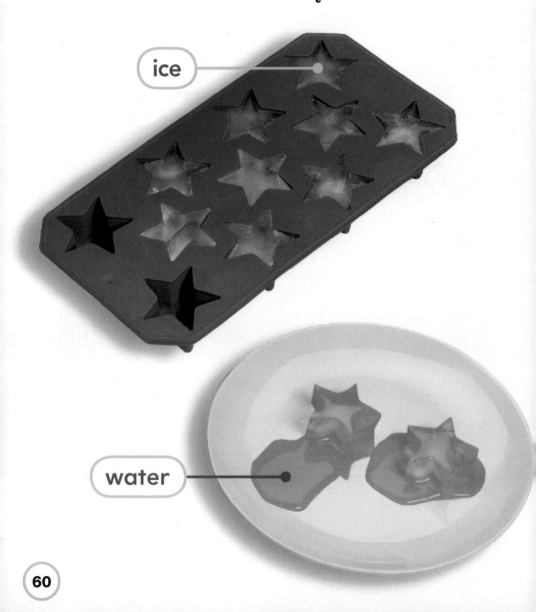

ice

water

Water changes when the weather changes.
Water can change into ice when it is cold.
Ice can change into water when it is warm.

Compare

What is different about water and ice? What is the same?

2 How Does Temperature Change Water?

Water in clouds will freeze
when the air is cold.
Different kinds of ice fall
from clouds.
Snow is ice that falls
from clouds.
Snow is white and soft.

snow

Sleet is another kind of ice
that falls from clouds.
Sleet is frozen rain mixed
with snow.
Sleet is wet.

sleet

Ice in Warm Weather

Ice can fall from clouds
when it is warm.
Hail is round ice and hard snow.
Hail falls during thunderstorms.
Hail can be small or big.

hail

High in the clouds
air can be cold.
Water in clouds can turn to ice.
Hail falls from clouds.

Classify

Is hail a solid or a liquid?

Glossary

freeze To change from a liquid to a solid. When water freezes, it changes to ice.

hail Round ice and hard snow.

melt To change from a solid to a liquid. When ice melts, it changes back to water.

Glossary

rain Water that falls in drops from clouds.

sleet Frozen rain mixed with snow.

snow Ice that falls from clouds. Snow is white and soft.

Responding

**Think About What
You Have Read**

1 To change from a solid
to a liquid is to _____.
A) freeze
B) melt
C) snow

2 How are rain and snow
different?

3 When will ice melt?

4 It is hot and cloudy.
Will it rain or snow? Why?

Plants

Contents

1 What Are the Parts of Plants?

Plants have parts.
Plants have roots, stems, and leaves.
Some plants have flowers.
Each part helps in a different way.

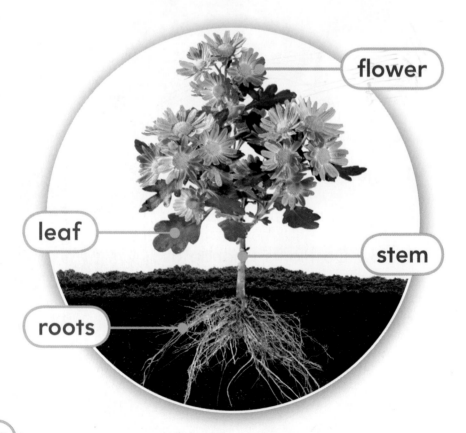

flower

leaf

stem

roots

Roots and Stems

Roots take in water.
Roots hold the plant
in the ground.
A **stem** joins parts of plants.
Stems carry water from the roots
to other parts.
Stems hold the plant up.

Leaves

Most plants have leaves.

Leaves make food for the plant.

Leaves also make oxygen.

People and animals need oxygen.

Flowers and Seeds

Many plants have flowers.

A **flower** makes seeds.

A **seed** has a new plant inside it.

New plants grow from seeds.

seeds

Draw Conclusions

Why are seeds important?

2 How Can Plants Be Sorted?

You can sort plants.

You can put plants in groups.

You can sort plants
by their parts.

Some plants have sharp points
called **spines**.

spines

Some plants have flowers.
Some plants have flat leaves.

flat leaf

Eating Plants

Some plants are food for people.
You can buy food plants
in a store.
These plants are safe to eat.
Not all plants are safe to eat.

Some plants are food for animals.

Draw Conclusions

How do plants help animals?

3 How Do Plants Change as They Grow?

Pine trees start as seeds.
Pine seeds are in a **cone**.
A seed grows into a plant
called a **seedling**.
The seedling grows into a tree.

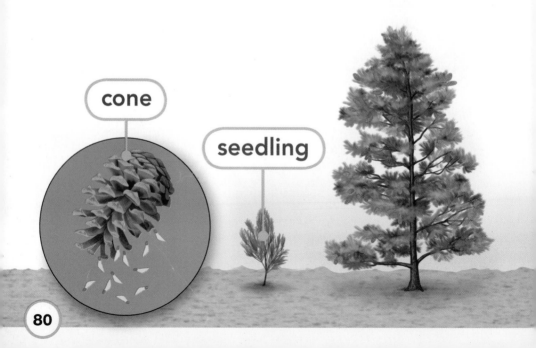

cone

seedling

The tree grows cones.
Seeds are in the cones.
Pine trees start as seeds!

Plant Life Cycles

Plants change as they grow. The order of changes that happen in the lifetime of a plant or animal is called a **life cycle**.

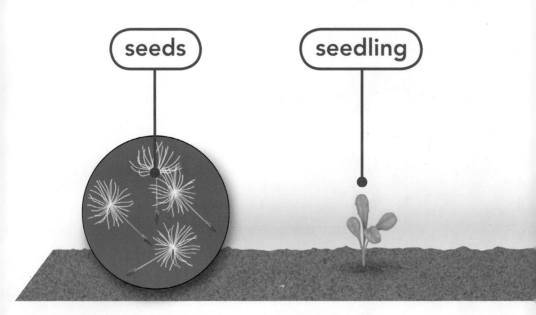

seeds

seedling

Plant Lives

Different plants have different
life cycles.
Some plants have long life cycles.
Some plants have short
life cycles.

Sequence

What comes after the seed
in a plant's life cycle?

growing
plant

flowers
grow

new
seeds

Glossary

cone The part of a pine tree where seeds grow.

flower The part of a plant that makes seeds.

leaf Part of a plant that makes food for the plant.

life cycle The order of changes that happen in the lifetime of a plant or animal.

roots The parts of the plant that take in water from the ground.

Glossary

seed The part of a plant that has a new plant inside it.

seedling A young plant.

spines Sharp points on a cactus.

stem Part of a plant that connects the roots to the other plant parts.

Think About What You Have Read

❶ A _____ makes seeds.

A) stem
B) flower
C) spine
D) root

❷ How do stems help a plant?

❸ What is one way to group plants?

❹ What happens in a plant's life cycle after it flowers?

Animals

Contents

1 How Do Animals Use Their Parts?

Animals have body parts. Some body parts help them find food.

Using Body Parts to Find Food

ears

eyes

legs and fingers

Some body parts help animals stay safe.
Some body parts help animals hide.

quills

stinger

color and shape

Parts for Moving

Animals have body parts
that help them move.
A bird has wings.
Wings help birds fly.
A bird has legs.
Legs help it walk and hop.
Legs help it hold on to trees.

wing

A fish has a tail and fins.
A tail and **fins** help fish move.
A lion has strong legs.
Strong legs help it run fast.

tail

fin

leg

Main Idea

How does a bird use its legs?

2 How Are Animals Grouped?

Scientists study animals.
They put animals into groups.

Mammals

One group is called mammals.
A baby **mammal** drinks milk
from its mother.
Most mammals have hair or fur.
Mammals have lungs.
Lungs help mammals breathe.

Birds and Fish

Another group is birds.

Birds have wings.

Birds have feathers.

Birds have lungs to breathe.

Another group is fish.

Fish live in water.

Most fish have scales.

Fish have gills.

Gills help fish breathe.

wing

scales

gills

Reptiles

Another group is reptiles.

A **reptile** has dry skin with scales.

Snakes are reptiles.

Lizards are reptiles.

lizard

Amphibians

Another group is amphibians.

An **amphibian** has wet skin.

It does not have hair or scales.

It does not have feathers.

Frogs are amphibians.

What Animals Eat

You can group animals
by what they eat.
Some animals eat plants.
These animals have flat teeth.
Some animals eat other animals.
These animals have sharp teeth.

flat teeth

sharp teeth

Compare and Contrast

How are the teeth of
animals different?

3 How Do Animals Grow and Change?

Living things change
as they grow.
The order of changes is called
a life cycle.
An **adult** is a full-grown
plant, animal, or person.

Life Cycle of a Salamander

eggs   ready to hatch

Adult animals can become parents. A new life cycle begins when an adult has babies.

Sequence

What part of a salamander's life cycle comes after the adult?

growing

adult

Glossary

adult A full-grown plant, animal, or person.

amphibian An animal that has wet skin with no hair, feathers, or scales.

fins Body parts that help a fish move.

gills Body parts that help a fish breathe under water.

Glossary

lungs Body parts that take in air.

mammal An animal that has hair or fur. A baby mammal drinks milk from its mother.

reptile An animal that has dry skin with scales.

wings Body parts that help animals fly.

Think About What You Have Read

❶ A mammal uses _____ to breathe.

A) wings

B) lungs

C) fins

D) gills

❷ How does a fish move?

❸ What is a full-grown animal called?

❹ How are fish and reptiles alike?

People

Contents

1 How Do People Use Their Parts?

People have many body parts.
You have five senses.
Your **senses** help you learn
about the world.
They help you smell and feel things.
They help you see and hear things.
They help you taste things.

You use your
hands to feel.

You use your
eyes to see.

You use your
ears to hear.

You use your
nose to smell.

You use your
mouth to taste.

109

Other Body Parts

Your body parts help you
do things.
You use your mouth to talk
and eat.

You use your legs to walk
and run.
You use your arms and hands
to hold.

Many animals have body parts
like yours.
A cat has eyes, ears, a nose,
a mouth, and legs.

ear

eye

leg

nose

A cat has paws.
You do not.
You have hands
and feet.

feet

Draw Conclusions

How do you think popcorn
feels, looks, and sounds?

2 How Do People Grow and Change?

People grow and change.

You were an **infant**, or baby.

Then you grew.

You kept growing.

You started going to school.

infant   toddler   school-age child

You will grow to be a teen.
A **teen** is a person between
13 and 19 years old.
Next, you will become an adult.

teen   adult   senior adult

People Need to Eat

You need to eat to stay healthy. Food gives you energy to live and grow.

Foods to Eat

Eat More of These Foods	Eat Less of These Foods

People Need to Exercise

You need to exercise to stay healthy.

Exercise is movement that keeps your body strong.

Running makes your body strong.
Jumping makes your body strong.

People Need to Sleep

You need to sleep to stay healthy.
You rest your body and mind
when you **sleep**.
You need about ten hours
of sleep each night.

Sequence

What do people grow to be
after they are teens?

Glossary

exercise Movement that keeps your body strong.

infant A new baby.

senses Sight, smell, hearing, touch, and taste. You can see, smell, hear, feel, and taste popcorn.

Glossary

sleep Rest for body and mind.

teen A person between 13 and 19 years old.

Think About What You Have Read

1 _____ is a movement that keeps your body strong.

A) Exercise

B) Infant

C) Sleep

D) Teen

2 For which of the senses do you use your nose?

3 How much sleep do you need?

4 What body parts help you play on a playground?

Living Things

Contents

1 What Is a Living Thing?

A **living thing** grows
and changes.
It makes other living things
that are like it.
It needs air and food.
It needs water and space.

People and animals
are living things.
Trees and grass
are living things, too.

Nonliving Things

A **nonliving thing** does not eat or drink.

It does not grow.

It does not make other things that are like it.

It does not need air, food, and water.

living thing

nonliving thing

A nonliving thing may
act like a living thing.
A fire grows.
A fire needs air.
But a fire does not need
food or water.
A fire is a nonliving thing.

Main Idea

What is a nonliving thing?

2 What Do Living Things Need?

Plants and animals need food. **Food** is what living things use to grow.

Plants make their own food. Plants use sunlight, air, and water to make food. **Sunlight** is energy from the Sun.

Food

Animals eat food.

Some animals eat plants.

Some animals eat other animals.

Many animals eat both plants and animals.

Most people eat both plants and animals.

Food Chain

Plants make their own food.

An insect eats plants.

A bird eats insects.

Water

Plants and animals need water.
Most plants get water
from the ground.

Some animals get water
from the food they eat.
Many animals get water
by drinking.

Air

Plants and animals need air.
Plants use air to make food.
Animals breathe in air.
Whales breathe air
just like you do.

whale

Space

Plants and animals need space.

Plants need space to grow.

Animals need space for a home.

Animals need space to find food.

Shelter

Animals need shelter.
Shelter is a safe place to live.
Some animals find shelter
in trees.

Classify

What do plants need to live?

Glossary

food What living things use to get energy.

living thing Something that grows, changes, and makes other living things like itself.

nonliving thing Something that does not eat, drink, grow, and make other things like itself.

shelter A safe place for animals to live.

sunlight Energy from the Sun.

Think About What You Have Read

❶ A _____ is a safe place for animals to live.

A) food

B) living thing

C) shelter

D) nonliving thing

❷ What do all living things need?

❸ How are nonliving things different from living things?

❹ Why is sunlight important?

Where Plants and Animals Live

Contents

1 What Lives in Forests?

A **forest** is a place
with many trees.
The trees grow close together.
Animals use the living things
in a forest.
Animals use the nonliving things
in a forest, too.
They use these things
for food and shelter.

bear

snake

blue jay

squirrel

plant

turtle

Other Kinds of Forests

There are many kinds of forests.
Some are hot and wet.
Some are cold and dry.
This forest is cold.

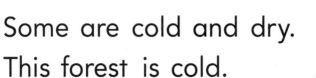

owl

Different kinds of plants live
in each forest.
Different kinds of animals live
in each forest.
This forest is wet.

parrot

Main Idea

Are all forests the same?
Tell why or why not.

2 What Lives in Oceans and Wetlands?

An **ocean** is a large body
of salty water.
An ocean is not a living thing.
An ocean has many living things
in it.
Some animals live in the ocean.
Some animals live
near the ocean.

whale

jellyfish

Ocean animals have
special parts.
These parts help them live
in water.
Fish have fins and tails to swim.
Fish have gills to breathe.

shark

tail

fin

gills

A Wetland

A **wetland** is low land
that is very wet.
There is water in a wetland.
Sometimes the water is salty.
Sometimes the water is not salty.

There is mud in a wetland.
There are plants
in a wetland, too.

There are many kinds of animals
in a wetland.
The animals find food and water
in the mud, water, and plants.
They find shelter in the mud,
water, and plants.

heron

snail

alligator

hawk

panther

mosquito

Compare and Contrast

How are oceans different from wetlands?

153

3 What Lives in a Desert?

A **desert** is a place
with very little water.
It is not easy to live in a desert.
It can be hard to find food.
It can be hard to find water.

lizard

It is hot during the day.
It is cool at night.
Many animals sleep
during the day.
They look for food
at night.

fox

saguaro

scorpion

Living in Deserts

Desert plants and animals have special parts.
The parts help them live in dry places.
A cactus has thick stems.
It has waxy skin.
The stems and skin hold water.

cactus

A camel has wide feet.
Its feet help it walk in sand.

Draw Conclusions

**Why do many desert animals
sleep during the day?**

Glossary

desert A place with very little water.

forest A place with many trees that grow close together.

ocean A large body of salty water.

wetland A low area of land that is very wet.

Think About What You Have Read

❶ A large body of salty water is called _____.

   A) a wetland

   B) an ocean

   C) a desert

   D) a forest

❷ What helps a cactus hold water?

❸ Where do wetland animals find food, water, and shelter?

❹ How are all forests alike?

Magnets

Contents

1 What Are Magnets?

A **magnet** is an object that attracts some metal objects.
Attract means pull toward each other.
Magnets come in many shapes.
They come in many sizes.
They have many uses.

magnet

An object that attracts magnets
is **magnetic**.
A metal called iron is magnetic.
A metal called steel is magnetic.
Most magnetic objects have iron
or steel in them.

magnetic objects

An object that does not attract
magnets is not magnetic.
Glass and wood objects are
not magnetic.
Neither are paper objects.
Metal objects that do not have iron
or steel are not magnetic.
These objects do not attract
magnets.

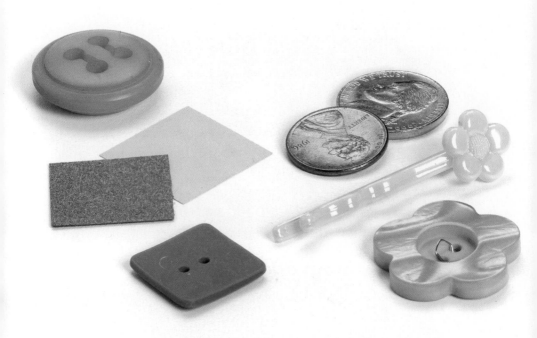

These objects are not magnetic.

Magnets Act on Each Other

Magnets have forces that act on other magnets.

The force can be a push.

It can be a pull.

Magnets have two poles.

The **poles** are where the forces are strongest.

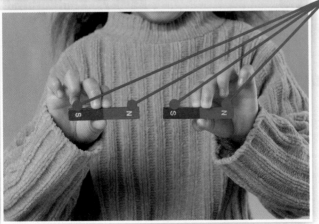

poles

Some magnets have letters
on the poles.
N is for north pole.
S is for south pole.
Poles with the same
letter are like poles.
Like poles repel each other.
Repel means to push away.
Poles with different letters
are unlike poles.
Unlike poles attract.

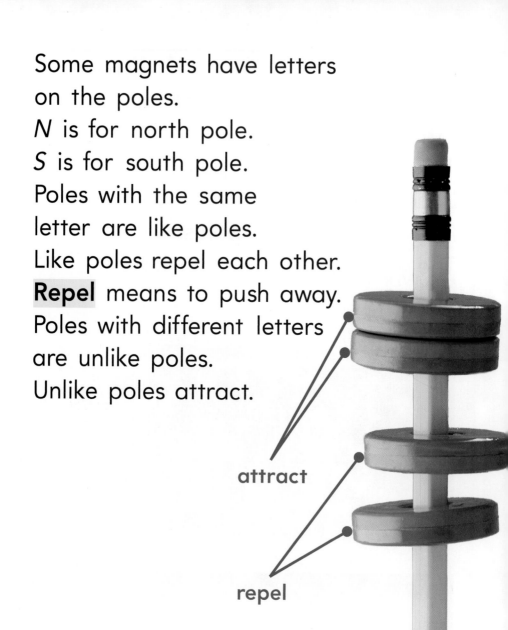

attract

repel

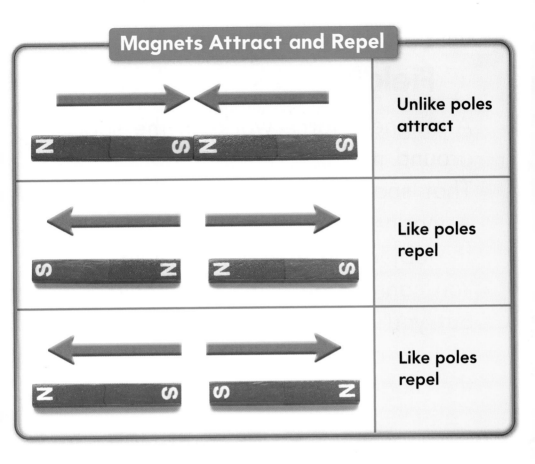

	Unlike poles attract
	Like poles repel
	Like poles repel

Magnets Attract and Repel

Cause and Effect

What happens when like poles are together?

2 What Is a Magnetic Field?

A magnet's force works in the space around it.
That space is its **magnetic field**.
A magnet can attract or repel only the objects in its magnetic field.
You cannot see a magnetic field.
But you can find it by looking at how objects are attracted to the magnet.

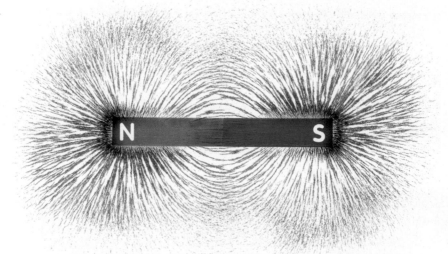

These are little pieces of iron. They are attracted to the magnet's poles. They show where the magnetic field is.

A magnet's force is strongest at its poles. The magnet does not need to touch objects to attract them. The force is so strong that a magnet can attract things without touching them!

Magnetic objects are pulled to the poles. That is where the force is strongest.

Compare and Contrast

How is the center of a magnet different from the poles?

3 How Strong Is a Magnet's Force?

The pushing or pulling force of a magnet is its **magnetic force**. Magnetic force can make an object move without touching it. Magnetic force acts on magnetic objects. It acts on other magnets, too.

These objects are pulled to the magnets by a magnetic force.

A magnet's force can attract objects through other things.
Objects can be attracted through paper and glass.
They can be attracted through plastic, water, and air, too.

Magnets work through pictures.

Magnets work through air.

Magnets work through plastic.

Magnets work through glass and water.

Weakening a Magnet's Force

Magnetic force gets weaker as the object moves away from the magnet. A strong magnet can attract an object from far away.
A weak magnet can only attract objects that are close.

Magnets work through paper.

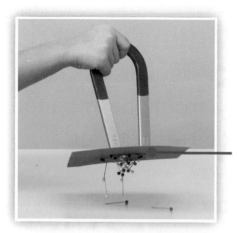 one piece of paper

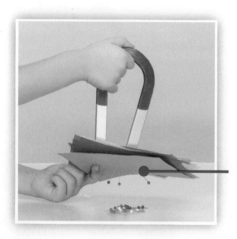 many pieces of paper

This magnet's force can pass through one piece of paper. It is too weak to pass through many pieces of paper.

Draw Conclusions

How can a magnet hold a picture to a refrigerator?

Glossary

attract When objects pull toward each other.

magnet An object that attracts iron or steel objects.

magnetic An object that is attracted by a magnet.

magnetic field The space around a magnet where the magnet's force works.

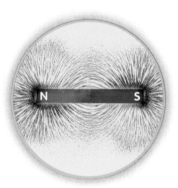

Glossary

magnetic force The pushing or pulling force of a magnet.

poles The places on a magnet where the forces are strongest.

repels When a magnet pushes an object away from itself.

Responding

Think About What You Have Read

❶ The space around a magnet where the magnet's force works is its _____.

A) poles
B) magnetic force
C) magnetic field

❷ How should you hold two magnets so they pull toward each other?

❸ Where on a magnet is the force strongest?

❹ Predict what will happen if you put a magnet near a pile of steel paper clips.

Caring for
Our Earth

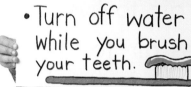

• Turn off water while you brush your teeth.

• Use paper and plastic bags more than one time.

• Write or draw on both sides of paper.

Contents

1 How Do We Use Air?

Air is a natural resource.
People need air to live.
Animals need air to live.
Plants need air to live, too.
This boy uses air to
blow bubbles.

People use air in many ways.
You use air to cool off
on a hot day.
This boat uses air
to move across water.

Air Pollution

Air pollution happens when harmful things get into the air. Dust and smoke are pollution. Dust comes from many places. Smoke comes from fires. Pollution can make living things sick.

air pollution

clean air

Clean air helps living things stay healthy.
Clean air keeps buildings and other things clean.
Pollution makes things dirty.
This man is cleaning up pollution.

Draw Conclusions

Why is air important?

2 How Do We Use Water?

Water is a natural resource.
People need water to live.
You use water to drink.
You use water to wash.
You use water
to cook and clean.

People use water in other ways.
You use water to swim
and have fun.
People use water to put out fires.

Water Pollution

Water pollution happens when harmful things get into water. Trash in water is a harmful thing. Oil in water is a harmful thing. Pollution can make living things sick.

cleaning oil off a bird

water pollution

People can help
clean up pollution.
They can pick up trash.
They can stop putting it
into the water.

Classify

What are three ways
people use water?

3 How Can We Help Earth?

You can help save natural resources.

Reuse

You can **reuse**, or use something again. Resources last longer when you reuse.

tire swing

tire sandals

Think about what you can reuse.
Plant flowers in a milk carton.
Use pictures in old magazines
to make cards.
Watts Towers reuse tiles,
metal, and glass.

Recycle

You can recycle.

A new object is made

when you **recycle**.

You can recycle many things.

You can recycle paper.

You can recycle plastic.

plastic bottles

backpack

This is what happens
when you recycle cans.
First, you recycle some cans.
Next, old cans are made
into new cans.
Last, you use the new cans.

old cans

new cans

Reduce

You can **reduce**, or use less of something.
Look at the picture.
How can you reduce what you use?

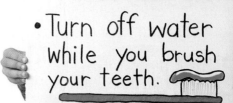

- Turn off water while you brush your teeth.
- Use paper and plastic bags more than one time.
- Write or draw on both sides of paper.

Sequence

What happens when things are recycled?

Glossary

air pollution Harmful things that get into the air.

recycle To take an object and make a new object from it.

reduce To use less of something.

- Turn off water while you brush your teeth.
- Use paper and plastic bags more than one time.
- Write or draw ~th sides

Glossary

reuse To use something again. Watts Towers reuse tiles, metal, and glass.

water pollution Harmful things that get into water.

Think About What You Have Read

1 What happens when harmful things get in water?

A) recycle

B) reduce

C) reuse

D) water pollution

2 What are two ways that people use air?

3 What happens when you reduce?

4 What might happen if we do not take care of Earth's resources?

Glossary

A

adult A full-grown plant, animal, or person.

air pollution Harmful things that get into the air.

amphibian An animal that has wet skin with no hair, feathers, or scales.

attract When objects pull toward each other.

C

cloud Many drops of water together.

Glossary

cone The part of a pine tree where seeds grow.

D

desert A place with very little water.

E

exercise Movement that keeps your body strong.

F

fall The season that follows summer. In fall, the weather gets cooler.

fins Body parts that help a fish move.

Glossary

flower The part of a plant that makes seeds.

food What living things use to get energy.

forest A place with many trees that grow close together.

freeze To change from a liquid to a solid. When water freezes, it changes to ice.

G

gills Body parts that help a fish breathe under water.

Glossary

hail Round ice and hard snow.

infant A new baby.

leaf Part of a plant that makes food for the plant.

life cycle The order of changes that happen in the lifetime of a plant or animal.

Glossary

living thing Something that grows, changes, and makes other living things like itself.

lungs Body parts that take in air.

(M)

magnet An object that attracts iron or steel objects.

magnetic An object that is attracted by a magnet.

magnetic field The space around a magnet where the magnet's force works.

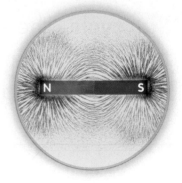

Glossary

magnetic force The pushing or pulling force of a magnet.

mammal An animal that has hair or fur. A baby mammal drinks milk from its mother.

melt To change from a solid to a liquid. When ice melts, it changes back to water.

Moon A space object close to Earth.

nonliving thing Something that does not eat, drink, grow, and make other living things like itself.

Glossary

ocean A large body of salty water.

planet A space object the moves around the Sun.

poles The places on a magnet where the forces are strongest.

rain Water that falls in drops from clouds.

Glossary

recycle To take an object and make a new object from it.

reduce To use less of something.

repels When a magnet pushes an object away from itself.

reptile An animal that has dry skin with scales.

reuse To use something again. Watts Towers reuse tiles, metal, and glass.

Glossary

roots The parts of the plant that take in water from the ground.

rotates Spins. Day and night happen when Earth rotates.

S

season A time of year that has its own kind of weather.

seed The part of a plant that has a new plant inside it.

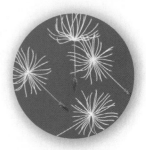

seedling A young plant.

Glossary

senses Sight, smell, hearing, touch, and taste. You can see, smell, hear, feel, and taste popcorn.

shadow Something that forms when and object blocks light.

shelter A safe place for animals to live.

sleep Rest for body and mind.

sleet Frozen rain mixed with snow.

snow Ice that falls from clouds. Snow is white and soft.

Glossary

spines Sharp points on a cactus.

spring The season that follows winter. Many baby animals are born in spring.

star A space object that makes its own light.

stem Part of a plant that connects the roots to the other plant parts.

summer The season that follows spring. Summer is the warmest season.

Sun The brightest space object in the day sky.

Glossary

sunlight Energy from the Sun.

T

teen A person between 13 and 19 years old.

temperature How warm or cool something is. The temperature is cold when there is snow.

thermometer A tool that measures temperature.

W

water cycle Water moving from Earth to the sky and back again.

Glossary

water pollution Harmful things that get into water.

weather What the air outside is like.

wetland A low area of land that is very wet.

wings Body parts that help animals fly.

winter The season that follows fall. Winter is the coldest season.

Index

A

Adult, 100–101, 115

Air

living things need for, 126, 136

pollution of, 182–183

uses for, 180–181

warmed by the Sun, 6

Air pollution, 182–183

Amphibians, 98

Animals, 47, 49

body parts of, 90–93, 112–113, 149

of deserts, 154–155, 156, 157

as food, 132–133

food for, 79, 99, 130, 132–133

of forests, 144–147

groups of, 94–98

life cycle of, 100–101

as living things, 127

moving, 92–93

in and near oceans, 148–149

needs of, 130, 132–138, 180

seasons and, 43, 45, 47, 49

staying safe, 91

ways to breathe, 95, 96, 149

ways to move, 92–93

of wetlands, 152–153

Arms, 111

Attract, 162–174

B

Birds, 4, 92, 96

Credits